IN GOD'S CREATION

DEVOTIONS FOR THE BEACH

IN GOD'S CREATION

DEVOTIONS FOR THE BEACH

BARBARA BARANOWSKI

WESTBOW
PRESS®
A DIVISION OF THOMAS NELSON
& ZONDERVAN

WestBow Press books may be ordered through booksellers or by contacting:

WestBow Press
A Division of Thomas Nelson & Zondervan
1663 Liberty Drive
Bloomington, IN 47403
www.westbowpress.com
1 (866) 928-1240

ISBN: 978-1-9736-3360-0 (sc)
ISBN: 978-1-9736-3361-7 (e)

Library of Congress Control Number: 2018908025

Print information available on the last page.

WestBow Press rev. date: 07/23/2018

Dedicated to:

My Lord and Savior Jesus Christ, my wonderful husband
John—the best beach buddy ever, our lovely daughters and
their delightful families with whom we have enjoyed many
hours of beach fun, and my parents, for teaching me a love
of the outdoors and an appreciation for God's creation.

Introduction

WHETHER WE SIP our morning coffee from the deck of a beach cottage or at the edge of the surf, the splendor of God's creation begs us to slow down and enjoy the beautiful coastal gift He has provided. Each wave sounds out God's declaration of existence. The seashore beckons us, and we are forever transformed. Its peacefulness erases stress, and our spirit is taken to a place of tranquility. Our memories linger on, long after our footprints and sandcastles are gone. We long again for colorful morning skies with hues of orange and pink and the sun's warmth to ease the chill of winter days. We recall the invigorating coolness of salty breezes as hungry cries of seagulls fill the air, and we look forward to the day we can return to the seawater's soothing cure and the sand's restorative power.

This is a devotional book for anyone wishing to draw nearer to God in praise and worship while enjoying time at the beach or when dreaming of being there. Have a great day and listen to God's voice reminding you that He loves you.

The earth is the Lord's, and the fullness thereof;
the world, and they that dwell therein.
Psalm 24:1 (KJV)

Contents

God's Sovereignty

Then they cried out to the Lord in their trouble, and he brought them out of their distress. He stilled the storm to a whisper; the waves of the sea were hushed.
Psalm 107:28-29

"THE WEATHER FORECAST looks good for this week," I told my husband as we packed for our beach trip. When we plan so far ahead we know weather is a gamble. But I pictured how the perfect day would go. I awaken to the caress of sunbeams and their heat provides a sauna, while the cool breeze wicks the moisture from my skin. A dip in the ocean's warm, salty water massages away winter's tension. My mind empties as I live in the present, and to-do lists fade away. Now, this is what I call a day at God's perfect spa.

However, darkening skies may unveil another scene if threatening weather rolls in. We hope that warning flags and gale force warnings will not announce an angry storm surge. But should that day unfold, we are prepared with books, movies, and indoor games. We watch as the storm unveils God's great and infinite power through the wind and waves. In our spirit, we hear Jesus commanding, "Peace, be still," and we are delighted when the sun returns.

No matter the weather, every day at the beach reminds us of God's sovereignty over His creation. As the wind calls forth its energy and whitecaps clap a rhythmic chant, we hear their declaration, "Listen carefully. Hear it? Our Creator is in control."

Whether our day is calm and relatively stress free, or one that makes the angriest waves look tame, God brings peace to our heart and quiet to our soul, if we seek Him.

Lord over all of life, I know that because You love me, You will be with me, no matter what my day brings— sunshine or storm. Be in charge of this day, and help me to yield my will to Yours.

REFLECTIONS

_____

_____

_____

_____

_____

_____

_____

_____

_____

_____

_____

_____

_____

_____

_____

_____

_____

_____

_____

_____

_____

_____

Just Jump In!

Mightier than the thunder of the great waters, mightier than the breakers of the sea—the Lord on high is mighty. Psalm 93:4

IT WAS THE beginning of summer. Anxiously our family had awaited the rolling waves, warm sand, and lazy days at the beach. I had forgotten, however, how nippy the early summer water is before the sun's sustaining warmth dispels the iciness of winter's sojourn. Running full speed, I could hardly wait for the salty breakers to wash over me, carrying my cares and worries out to sea. How could I resist as the waves applauded my arrival. It wasn't long, though, before I made a hasty retreat and waited until the noonday heat warmed the water.

It is like that with our spirit, chilled by setbacks. There is remedy as we trust in God. The warmth of His love overwhelms our spirit, leaving us free to jump into life again. In Hebrews 13:5 we read, "Never will I leave you; never will I forsake you," referring to God's steadfast devotion. By sending Jesus to be our Savior and the Holy Spirit to lead us into truth, He demonstrates His love and concern for our needs.

Are you discouraged today? Does it seem like you have been plunged into frigid waters of fear, disappointment, and despair? God is waiting to hear from you. Talk to Him today and see how much He loves you. What are you waiting for? Just jump in!

Thank You most gracious Father that You celebrate when we turn to You. Like the pounding waves upon the surf, You clap with joy because of Your great love for us which warms even the coldest heart.

REFLECTIONS

Free to Run

*The name of the Lord is a fortified tower; the righteous
run to it and are safe.* Proverbs 18:10

I COULD HARDLY wait to walk up and over the sand
dunes when we arrived at the beach. The swaying, golden
sea oats waved their greeting to me with their long, slender
stalks. The fragile beach roses and delicate pink ground-
geraniums made my entrance as regal as a movie star on
the red carpet. Once at the rounded peak, my seven year-
old eyes could see far down the beach and were drawn
wondrously to the wide expanse of white, crystal sand. I was
breathless with amazement as I realized that I now stood at
the edge of my country. The pounding, rolling waves invited
me to run with effortless abandon toward them. My father
slipped his hand from mine, and I dashed off joyfully and
freely—anticipating the briny aroma and salty happiness
that awaited me.

In times of distress and disappointment I run to Jesus,
my Strong Tower, with the same fervor as I ran to the water's
edge. Our verse reminds me also, that we who know the

Lord are free to run to His safety and security even when our days are routine, and joy is ours. In the fortress of His love we find peace. I need that daily. Don't you?

Lord, remind me often to have the same urgency for Your strength and protection in life's sunlit days as I have in the thunderous storms that come without warning. You are my High Tower where I find refuge. Thank You that I can meet You there every day.

REFLECTIONS

Like a Sweet Fragrance

For we are to God the pleasing aroma of Christ among those who are being saved and those who are perishing,
2 Corinthians 2:15

COULD YOU RECOGNIZE the ocean if you were sight or hearing impaired? Could you identify it by scent? Close your eyes and breathe in the beach bouquet. You can smell the seaside even before you walk over a sand dune. Fragrant memories, often still sensually powerful once you leave, greet you: the salty smell of the ocean's presence, seaweed's iodine-like odor, coconut-infused sunscreen, and the brininess of shellfish. Along the beach, the wind kicks up the scent of damp sand and vegetation. We get an idea of how busy and unique this place is, as we breathe in its charm.

Have you ever thought of yourself as being a pleasing aroma to God? Paul reminds us, as he did the believers in Corinth, that when we are in Christ we delight God. Later Paul wrote to the Ephesians, "Christ loved us and gave himself up for us as a fragrant, sacrificial offering to God" (Ephesians 5:2). The only way to please God is to accept

Jesus' sacrifice for our sins and then live for Him in the presence of others.

Would others recognize us as the sweet fragrance of Christ if we entered a room? Are they drawn to Him through us? We can answer "yes" to both if we spend time with Him.

Dear Jesus, thank You for loving us and giving Yourself for our sins as a fragrant offering to God, our Father. May we be the same to those who are lost and perishing without You.

REFLECTIONS

Surf's Up

Then we will no longer be infants, tossed back and forth by the waves, and blown here and there by every wind of teaching and by the cunning and craftiness of people in their deceitful scheming. Ephesians 4:14

UP AND RIDE, lose balance, tumble in crashing waves, and the sequence repeats until the surfer catches a powerful wave and rides all the way to shore. We watch at daybreak as the lone teen paddles out over and over, seeking propulsion for a thrilling ride. While the sun rises higher and the onshore winds dominate, a few more join in. When the surfers are no longer alone in the water, they tiredly pull themselves onto the sand and wait for sunset. Sometimes these thrill seekers ride after a storm, looking for that enormous tidal push. Although they may be experienced, reading the waves and executing perfect timing is crucial. At the end of their day, they unleash their boards and head home to recount the "reels"—surfer term for the lasting, exhilarating rides they've had.

Sometimes we reel from circumstances that, unlike

the surfer, do not make us ecstatic. We are dashed against life's shore by swells of hurt, loss, and discouragement. We may drag upon the sand of life, physically and spiritually exhausted. But in His constant care, God is in our midst when life is tumbling out of control. He gives us strength to stay the course, ride the swells, and approach the shore. Then lovingly, He places us on solid ground again.

Philippians 4:7 promises that God's peace transcends our understanding. When we are in a right relationship with Him, we give Him control over every situation. Then in return we have a peace that doesn't depend on a perfect ride through life. We are not alone because with God there is never a wipeout.

Lord, sometimes the waves of life overtake me, and my spirit struggles to stay afloat. I thank You that on those days You are there, holding my head up and reminding me that I am of extreme value to You. Thank You, too, that in Your timing You place me gently on solid ground.

REFLECTIONS

Renting a Color

Praise the Lord, my soul. Lord my God, you are very great; you are clothed with splendor and majesty.
Psalm 104:1

WALK ALONG THE beach and notice the colorful houses and condos—some small and charming, others large and stately. Regardless of size or color, their tranquil presence and beauty represents freedom and release from daily deadlines and frustrations. Each presents a contrast to the natural earthy hues of beach landscape, with colors like sky blue, sea foam green, seashell pink, or sunshine yellow.

God's artistry also lets us experience His brushstrokes of beauty along the seashore and the symphony of ocean waves as they lull the tired to sleep. The blue-green water, bringing forth multi-colored shells, sea glass, and stones, sings back to each dwelling, "I display God's greatness, and you are the colorfully framed edge of this beautiful picture. We are all here to glorify Him."

God is the ultimate Creator and Builder. Nothing we build can compare. No matter the size, color, or style of the lodging where we hang our beach towels, it is a place to worship God's magnificence with all of creation. Man constructs the imperfect; but our perfect God spoke into existence the beauty of the seas (Genesis 1:9). A beach dwelling may take us to the majestic water's edge, but daily our Lord wants to immerse us in His ocean of love.

Dear God, we praise You for Your majestic creation and Your great love for us. Through Jesus You have provided a way for us to one day be with You in the indescribable glory of heaven. We acknowledge that You are the Creator and Supplier of all we need. Thank You for allowing us to experience You in the beauty of this place.

REFLECTIONS

Ocean Breeze

Then he climbed into the boat with them, and the wind died down. They were completely amazed. Mark 6:51

"THANK GOODNESS WE have this breeze. We won't swelter today in the hot sun," I declare to my husband from under my beach umbrella. We love the beach despite some days of scorching heat and blistering sand. This day the wind hugs me with a gentle caress, and I enjoy the comfort it brings. However, I remember those times when the wind is angry and violent, as a tropical storm or hurricane approaches.

Writers of the New Testament document stories of Jesus and windy conditions, as well. Mark's gospel relates how Jesus rescued the disciples caught on the Sea of Galilee, also called Lake of Gennesaret. Although the Sea of Galilee is small, the difference in height between the seacoast and surrounding mountains triggers great temperature changes. Suddenly, fierce winds are funneled directly to the center of the lake, causing treacherous storms and perilous waves for fishing boats caught without warning.

We know our lives contain winds of change, just as sudden and difficult to manage. We may rejoice in blessings blown our way, but sometimes an angry tempest of discomfort, sorrow, or difficulty blasts into our life and leaves us longing for a gentle breeze of relief. In Acts, the Holy Spirit's presence is described as a rushing mighty wind (Acts 2:2). The Holy Spirit's mighty presence is able to calm the roughest of waters. As Jesus is our Savior, the Holy Spirit is our weather tamer, as He aids, comforts, and strengthens us. He is our Friend who helps us bare our burdens and walk through any storm. Feel His presence as you approach the day.

Dear Lord, I long for the relief that only You bring. I give everything I am to You and gladly welcome the work of Your Holy Spirit in my life today. Thank you for every refreshing breeze You send my way.

REFLECTIONS

Rip Currents

No temptation has overtaken you except what is common to mankind. And God is faithful; he will not let you be tempted beyond what you can bear. But when you are tempted, he will also provide a way out so that you can endure it. 2 Corinthians 10:13

RED FLAGS UNFURL along the beach as they scream forth frantic warnings—unsafe to swim, beware of danger! A beautiful day at the beach is interrupted by rip currents, powerful ocean channels that run from the beach into the ocean. Because they can be deadly, lifeguards warn surfers and swimmers of the hazardous conditions and caution them to return to shore. If a swimmer forgets how to react and is overpowered, a rescuer throws out a floating lifeline.

Because God loves us, He sends forth a warning, but with it comes the good news that Jesus is our Lifeline. In Romans 6:23 we read, "For the wages of sin is death, but the gift of God is eternal life in Christ Jesus our Lord." Revelation 22:12 addresses Jesus' second coming, "Look, I am coming soon! My reward is with me, and I will give to each person according to what they have done."

God is in the rescuing business. He sent Jesus to save us from raging emotional undercurrents. We may experience His warning flags through the Holy Spirit's counsel—situations we should avoid, paths we shouldn't go down, or decisions we must make. But He *will* provide a way when we cry out for help. He is faithful.

Heavenly Father, some days I feel overwhelmed by the undertow of daily survival. Remind me often that You are just a prayer away—even if "God, please help me," is all that I can utter. Thank You for the Holy Spirit Who steadfastly guards my life.

REFLECTIONS

The Right Covering

He will cover you with his feathers, and under his wings you will find refuge; his faithfulness will be your shield and rampart. You will not fear the terror of night, nor the arrow that flies by day. Psalm 91:4-5

BEACH UMBRELLAS LINE the sand, dotting the seashore with splashes of color and kaleidoscopic designs. They evoke a sense of leisurely, carefree days. My blue, yellow, and red-striped umbrella flaps gently in the wind, exclaiming, "hap-hap happy day," as I watch fellow beachgoers seek refuge as well from the sun's demanding rays.

However, there have been days when without warning the wind increases, and my essential sunshade becomes vulnerable—struggling to hold its spot. I hope it won't take flight, triggering an umbrella search and rescue operation.

Isn't life like that? Sometimes the winds blow gently across its fabric, allowing a day of simpler ease, with no more worries then what to wear to work or fix for dinner. Then suddenly, troubling winds accelerate, making a whirlwind of out-of-control circumstances, and we feel helpless as we wonder where our emotions will land. We feel exposed and vulnerable, running to capture control and security again.

Unlike the unpredictability of our temporary beach sunshade, we have an all-sufficient, always dependable Covering for our lives. When we accept Jesus Christ as our Savior and Lord, He becomes our Covering from the shifting winds of life's difficulties. When we trust Him by faith we don't have to chase after Him; He is steadfast and firmly planted. Today, rest under the canopy of His love and be enveloped in His promises for your life.

Lord, thank You that every day I am under Your mighty covering and Your wings of protection. Because of You I need not fear what this world brings. As You are faithful to me every moment, please let me be faithful to You.

REFLECTIONS

Hidden Treasure

*And if you look for it as for silver and search for it as for hidden treasure, then you will understand the fear of the L*ORD *and find the knowledge of God.* Proverbs 2:4-5

MY HUSBAND LOVES to metal detect with our young grandchildren in morning's fresh air. They look for a "treasure" that has eluded others. "Papa, maybe we will find something valuable today," Andrew declared one morning when the two went out. He anticipated the steady, high-pitched "beep, beep, beep," of the metal detector, or the lucky wand, as he called it.

"Listen, it is sounding," John said, and they impatiently scooped the layers of sand into the sifter and carefully parted grains for the big reveal. Of course, most times, the only things exposed are soda pop tops or coins. But with small children, coins are a treasure. Older ones like to dig a little deeper for the jewelry they might find. And so the hunt continued until Andrew's pockets jingled with his "wealth."

Jesus often taught about treasure. He reminds us to seek

treasure that fills the deep longing in our heart. Some scratch the surface and settle for far less than we are promised, while others dig deeper to unlock the precious riches of His word. Why settle for a few mere coins when you can have every treasure in His storehouse? Seek today and you will be thrilled at what you find.

Lord, remind me often to search for the treasure that only You provide. Let Your Word be more valuable to me than anything the world offers.

REFLECTIONS

_____

_____

_____

_____

_____

_____

_____

_____

_____

_____

_____

_____

_____

_____

_____

_____

_____

At The Water's Edge

*Who is like you, L*ORD *God Almighty? You, L*ORD*, are mighty, and your faithfulness surrounds you. You rule over the surging sea; when its waves mount up, you still them.* Psalm 89:8-9

I ENJOY SITTING at the water's edge when the tide is out. The waves lap the shore with a gentle, comfortable cadence, allowing me to move my chair closer to its grandeur. It seems peaceful as the rhythmic waves break gently on the shoreline, giving the sand a reprieve from the pounding surf.

Gratefully, sometimes we get a break from the turbulence of daily living—a time when we enjoy a gentler pace of life. The day has a familiar beat and order to it. But other times we are pounded with powerful waves of uncertainty that pummel relentlessly until we feel we cannot stand in their midst. It is then that we need the only One Who is able to calm the tide.

Psalm 93:4 reminds us that the Lord is mightier than the breakers of the sea, and He enfolds us in His loving arms like the waters envelope the ocean's depths. He can handle all our times—the ebb and the flow, the calm and the fury. In our verse today we are reminded that when our life is His, we can approach the water's edge with confidence, no matter how high the waves are. Walk with Him today. He waits there for you there.

Heavenly Father, thank You for walking with me through times of peace and days of trials. Help me feel your Holy Spirit gently reminding me that You are near.

REFLECTIONS

_____

_____

_____

_____

_____

_____

_____

_____

_____

_____

_____

_____

_____

_____

_____

_____

_____

_____

Windsurfing

The wind blows wherever it pleases. You hear its sound, but you cannot tell where it comes from or where it is going. So it is with everyone born of the Spirit. John 3:8

THE WIND—GOD'S ENERGY for windsurfers. This day was perfect, as I enjoyed watching their sport that combines surfing and sailing. I thought about how wonderful it must be to "fly" across the waves. Some rides were short. But then an experienced surfer would set sail, seemingly caught in time and space, concentrating on the course. It was a thrill to watch the intimate relationship between surfer, sail, wind, and water, although the challenge was unmistakable.

Our connection to God, our Creator, is like that. Although we would like to think we power our own lives, He has created all that we are and offers us an invitation to be in harmonic relationship with Him through the indwelling of the Holy Spirit.

In Genesis 1:2, we read that, "the Spirit of God was

hovering over the waters." Jesus promised in John 14:16-17, "I will ask the Father, and he will give you another advocate to help you and be with you forever—the Spirit of truth. The world cannot accept him, because it neither sees him nor knows him. But you will know him, for he lives with you and will be in you." So the Holy Spirit has been with us from the beginning and is with us now. If we are Christians, the Holy Spirit guides, comforts, counsels, and leads us into all truth.

Like the wind across the surfer's board, we cannot see the Holy Spirit with physical eyes, but we can experience Him. We are responsible to raise our sail of faith and allow Him to power us across life's waves. When we do that we will experience the ride of our life.

Dear God, I acknowledge that without the work of the Holy Spirit, I am powerless to accomplish Your will. Fill me now and use me as a vessel holy unto You.

REFLECTIONS

_____

_____

_____

_____

_____

_____

_____

_____

_____

_____

_____

_____

_____

_____

_____

_____

_____

_____

_____

_____

_____

Never Changing

Jesus Christ is the same yesterday and today and forever. Hebrews 13:8

FOR MANY OF us sunrise and sunset at the beach are favorite times of serenity and repose. As darkness births daylight, God's color palette, cooler air, and presence of newly beached shells delight the senses. Then with a silent farewell, the day winds down into a gentle nightfall, when even the most stressed among us finds peace from the frenetic pace of life.

Having that same quiet time with Jesus is like that. Maybe you are sitting on the sand or deck of a beach house. Look at the water and breathe in His glory. Let your prayer lift up His majesty, and the peace of the Holy Spirit soothe your mind and calm your spirit. Remember that He loves you more than the number of water drops in the ocean and grains of sand on the beach.

God spoke all of creation into existence and then told Moses in Exodus 3:14, "I am Who I Am," meaning "I was then, am now, and will be forever. I am constant and consistent." He had a perfect plan for us at conception, and it continues into eternity. He sent Jesus to save us from our sins and walk with us along the beach of life. Have you accepted His plan for your life? If you haven't asked Him to be your Savior, why not do that today. I would encourage you to turn to the Final Thoughts page to make that happen. If you have, rejoice in knowing that your every moment is in the Lord's hands.

Dear God, thank You for the beauty of a day on the beach, but especially for the beauty of the sunrise and sunset. Thank You, too, that You are the Great I Am, Who will never forsake me because You love me. May my life be hidden in Your perfect will.

REFLECTIONS

Casting Out

Casting all your care upon Him, for He cares for you.
1 Peter 5:7 (NKJV)

CATCHING A TROPHY fish—that is what I call a successful fishing experience. Cast out, wait, and reel in the prize. But I admit that when I fish for recreation, instead of catching a *mess* of fish, as my dad called a good haul, I just create a tangled mess of my line. So my experience is: cast out, wait, reel in knots, and lose my hook. I may even catch something quite unexpected—like a shoe or chair.

Isn't life like that sometimes? We cast out our hopes and dreams in life's ocean of aspirations, just knowing that we will catch something big—perhaps an enriching career, a wonderful marriage, the right education, or a perfect home. And then as we reel in our experiences, we find complicated, messy situations like divorce, financial struggle, job loss, illness, or death of loved ones. We either struggle to cast out again with renewed hope for a better catch, or attempt in our own strength to adapt to our changing situation.

The good news is God works more in our knotted

messes than we realize. He doesn't ask us to change before He helps. When we hurt, He hurts. When we cry out in pain, He reminds us that Jesus bore the pain of Calvary, so that we and our situations can be redeemed according to His will. Everything Jesus said becomes a practical reality for us.

Cast your care on the Lord, wait on His timing, and allow Him to reveal His plan. While you wait, pray and read the Bible. Learn of His mighty works. He is waiting to reveal them in your life. When you cast out with Jesus, your fishing line is in the Master's hands, and your catch is eternal.

Dear God, today I choose to cast all my anxieties and cares upon You, knowing that you love me. Thank You for the peace that You send when we trust our day to You,

REFLECTIONS

Sandpiper Dance

"Seek the Lord while he may be found; call on him while he is near." Isaiah 55:6

AH, THE JOYS of lazy beach days. I recline in my chair, expending only as much energy as needed to lift my water bottle, apply sunscreen, and move my eyes across the pages of my book. In contrast, I watch the boundless energy of the long-legged sandpipers, and their relatives, the shorter-legged sanderlings as they dance along the shore's edge. They move to and fro as they run toward the water, then retreat in haste—barely escaping an incoming wave. Their sharp eyes search for insects and crustaceans. They dart with urgency and remarkable coordination before the next wave can steal the sea's delicacy from their waiting beaks. And once again, their little legs carry them to the sand's safety. God provides sustenance for these charming, lively seashore birds.

As the foaming surf retreats, I think about my own urgencies of life, and how I give in to pressure, darting in and out of my activities like that sandpiper. Do I put my to-do list before seeking God? Isaiah 55:6 reminds us to seek the Lord today because tomorrow is not promised.

Today God waits for us to join Him at His banquet table with the same eagerness as the sandpiper seeks out its food. Tomorrow He will provide again. Let's slow down a bit and pull up a chair to enjoy the feast.

Heavenly Father, thank You for offering us refreshment and spiritual food for our hungering spirits. Thank You, too, that we don't have to dart around looking for You. You are constant and eager to serve us from Your table of blessings.

REFLECTIONS

In Rough Waters

A furious squall came up, and the waves broke over the boat, so that it was nearly swamped. Jesus was in the stern, sleeping on a cushion. The disciples woke him and said to him, "Teacher, don't you care if we drown?" He got up, rebuked the wind and said to the waves, "Quiet! Be still!" Mark 4:37-39

"LET'S GET DOWN to the beach early and set up our chairs and umbrella," I told my husband John. And I meant *really early*. My favorite time is just at sunrise. With coffee in hand I claim a spot and prepare for a full day of relaxation, reading, and writing. The waves roll moderately, and the seagull's cry wakes my senses. The deserted sand reveals its seaside real estate on which to stake my claim for the day. I delight in the way the shoreline has changed overnight with fresh shells from the night's breakers. The beach presents a fresh canvas every morning, while the waves sound forth their constant beat.

In contrast, as I pack up at day's end, I notice the change from morning. Beach activities have textured and rearranged the sand. Thunderous surf crashes closer, dashing intricate sandcastles. Sea foam encroaches upon my perfect spot, so I rescue my belongings and retreat.

Jesus spent three years of ministry around the Sea of Galilee. He knew its characteristics intimately. Squalls then and now arise suddenly, caused by difference in temperatures between the seacoast and mountains beyond. Tremendous swells and fierce winds cause danger to those caught on the water.

One evening a violent storm arose, striking fear in the disciples' hearts. Their tiny fishing boat was no match for the waves, so they called out in anguish to Jesus. The disciples thought that the Lord did not care about their safety. After all, He was sleeping in the midst of a storm. Jesus awoke, calmed the waves, and taught them again about putting their faith and trust in Him.

Have you ever been in unexpected breakers of life—with wave after wave of setbacks breaking upon your dreams or sweeping away your plans? Today, as on the Sea of Galilee, Jesus will take control with His calming, restorative power, if you will trust Him.

Jesus, Your Word stands the test when overwhelming tides of difficulty cause me to struggle. Remind me to move closer to You, knowing that You only can calm my fears and bring peace in the storm.

REFLECTIONS

_____

_____

_____

_____

_____

_____

_____

_____

_____

_____

_____

_____

_____

_____

_____

_____

_____

_____

_____

Beach Bags

Be filled with the Spirit. Ephesians 5:18

TOSSED ACROSS THE shoulder, beach bags almost shout with joy, "Watch me impress with my whimsical beauty." They show up in stores in early March, teasing and taunting us with their bright summer colors. They display their playfulness in graphic tropical and nautical designs. Their vivid imprints inaudibly boast that they love to be filled to overflowing with necessities and entertainment gear. They dare us to make delightful, lifetime memories. Once back at our dwelling at day's end, we unpack them, along with our stories, and make ready for the next morning.

The apostle Paul reminds us in Ephesians to be filled with the Spirit. What does that mean? The Bible says that believers in Jesus Christ have God's Spirit within them, but it seems that not all live a life utilizing His power. From the time we gave our life to Jesus, fruit of the Spirit qualities were planted within our own spirit. Paul relates in Galatians 5:22-23, "The fruit of the Spirit is love, joy, peace, forbearance, kindness, goodness, faithfulness, gentleness, and self-control." If we are attentive to cultivate these divine seeds in the garden of our heart, we experience the harvest, even through the trials of life. We are controlled by whatever occupies our thoughts and actions. As believers we inherit the indwelling of the Holy Spirit, but we determine the degree to which we allow Him control. When we are serious about yielding ourselves to God's will, we welcome all that He is.

As you fill your coffee cup and open your day with prayer, invite the Holy Spirit to bring a large yield of fruit in your life. Then when you take your colorful tote to the beach today, fill it with His abundance.

Lord, we desire Your presence with us every moment.
Remind us often that Your filling completes our day.

REFLECTIONS

Just Hold On

For I am the LORD your God who takes hold of your right hand and says to you, Do not fear; I will help you. Isaiah 41:13

SLOWLY THEY STROLLED hand in hand along the seashore searching for God's beach treasures. Every discovery was precious to the three-year old, as her tiny hand clutched a shell fragment. John, Ashley's grandfather, held tightly to the delicate fingers, protecting her from the power of an oncoming wave. The surf could certainly draw her away quickly if not for the protection of he who adored her.

Our walk with God is like that. We are His precious, beautiful treasures, in whom He delights to share the splendor of His kingdom. He longs to hold our heart in His hands, so we will not be swept away in the undercurrent of life's problems and perplexities. Yet, sometimes we pull free of His grasp to control our own pursuits without seeking His perfect plan. We purposely walk away from our Heavenly Father's protection and find ourselves in a precarious place where we never thought we would be. Once there we long for His strong hand to make our life right again.

There is great news! God longs to pick us up again and display us as His redeemed, if we repent of our sin. God sent Jesus to take the death penalty in our place.

In Him we experience forgiveness and everlasting love. Hold tightly to the nail-scarred hand of the One Who died for you. He *is* life's greatest Treasure.

Dear Jesus, thank You that I never walk alone because You walk with me and grasp my hand in Yours. Have control over my life as we walk the sands of life together.

REFLECTIONS

The Water That Heals

Whoever believes in me, as Scripture has said, rivers of living water will flow from within them." John 7:38

IT WAS ALMOST a calamity. A week before high school graduation our daughter Emily broke out with an extremely severe case of poison ivy. She had wandered into a dense patch while hanging out with friends. The ivy resin had left its burning, oozing marks and delivered its insufferable itch. Emily was miserable. Equally as unpleasant was the thought that she would walk across the stage at her graduation with white poison ivy lotion on to mask the redness and calm the itch. At least, she would match her white graduation gown.

We felt sorry for her, and even more so when she declared she would not go with her friends the next day to the beach, a graduation ritual in her school. I feared she would regret her decision. She had been in preschool and kindergarten with many of these friends, and now they would be going their separate ways.

"Why don't you reconsider?" I implored. "Salt water is known for healing the rash and itch of ivy. Just stay submerged," I said almost giggling, despite the seriousness of her situation. She gave in, resigned her fear, and went. And just as I suspected, Emily was greatly improved when she returned. The healing salt water had made a difference.

Water plays an important role in the Bible also. Jesus was baptized in the Jordan, walked on the Sea of Galilee, and told the Samaritan woman at the well in John 4:13-14, "Everyone who drinks this water will be thirsty again, but whoever drinks the water I give them will never thirst. Indeed, the water I give them will become in them a spring of water welling up to eternal life." What wonderful hope He offers to each of us. That is truly His healing water for our soul.

Thank You, Jesus, that You are the Water that quenches our spiritual thirst. You are the Fountain of Life. Remind us to drink deeply from Your Holy Spirit through prayer and study of Your word.

REFLECTIONS

Sea Glass Gems

The Lord your God has chosen you out of all the peoples on the face of the earth to be his people, his treasured possession. Deuteronomy 7:6

"ISN'T IT SAD the way some carelessly throw trash alongside the road?" I said to my husband as we headed to the beach. We dodged some broken amber glass while stopping to change drivers. Even with my complaining, I did not pick up the shards that were left. They were undesirable, unusable, shabby fragments of what they used to be.

But amazingly, if suddenly something half buried glimmered in the sand, I wouldn't hesitate to brush it off and marvel at its beauty. My attitude would be much different as I congratulate myself for retrieving a piece of polished, smooth glass. I would cherish this colorful gem, whether sparkling green, frosty white, or cobalt blue.

Sea glass is a rare treasure since at one time it had been a discarded bottle or jar in the ocean, instead of by the side of a highway. Then in creation's giant rock-tumbling waves, it was tossed and weathered before it reached the shore. It emerged transformed after surviving the turbulent surf and stormy winds. If the glass could tell of its epic journey, it might recount the pain of the tumult and rejoice at rescue. What was once debris with no intrinsic beauty is now a rare find, meant to become a beautiful piece of jewelry or craft art.

Sometimes we feel discarded, useless, and tempest-tossed by circumstances. However, God chose Israel to be His people, His treasure from Whom Jesus would come. And He sees us the same way—His treasure of great value. As with the glass, we might not realize our value, but He knows it. Take time today to submit your soul's fragments to the transforming power of Jesus. He will reveal the gem that you are.

Dear God, we thank You for being our Treasure and for creating us as Yours. Help us see how loved and desired we are in Your eyes.

REFLECTIONS

Take Flight

If I rise on the wings of the dawn, if I settle on the far side of the sea, even there your hand will guide me; your right hand will hold me fast. Psalm 139:9-11

THE COLORFUL BIRD-LIKE beauty soars, struggling to find its place in the wind's stream. I release my kite into the beach breeze, and it's almost like I take flight too. As I run for the launch, I look forward to the kite's dance when it catches the upward draft. My spirit rises as it stretches upward, and I guide it to a safe place among the other beautiful shapes and designs that I see already floating on high. I have set it free for a time, as it ascends to heights and becomes diminutive against the infinite deep blue sky. With a tug on the string, I know it is still aloft, and I can almost imagine it shouting down, "I'm here, still with you." I am happy that this day my kite launched successfully and flew among the clouds.

Our relationship with God is like that. He tugs at our heart, helping us find our place in the winds of life. The precious Holy Spirit is the power beneath and around us. Sometimes, as an uncontrolled kite plummets to the ground, so our lives do the same. As we struggle to rise, His love lifts us up and we soar once again. As with our kite God reminds us, "I'm here, still with you." Are you ready to rise in Him today?

Father God, help me hold on to You, as You hold fast to me. Remind me often that when You are in control, I can rise again when life disappoints. Thank you for the Holy Spirit Who controls my life.

REFLECTIONS

_____

_____

_____

_____

_____

_____

_____

_____

_____

_____

_____

_____

_____

_____

_____

_____

_____

_____

_____

_____

_____

Wonderfully Distinctive

For we are God's handiwork, created in Christ Jesus to do good works, which God prepared in advance for us to do. Ephesians 2:10

AS YOU WALK the seashore today pick up an assortment of shells on the beach and carefully observe the differences. If you have a magnifying glass, take it along. Notice the structural design, color, shape, and distinct pattern of each one. Some are ribbed while others are smooth. Did you pick up the spindle-shaped oyster drill? Perhaps you found the chalky round clam or a calico-striped scallop. The delicate, white angel wings are especially unique and charming. Every beautiful shell is a treasured gift from God, individually formed through heredity and environment. Some are quite rare, like the spiraled spotted scotch bonnet. Shells are celebrated in jewelry, décor, crafts, and clothing. Though different, each adds to the mosaic of the beach experience.

We are like that in God's kingdom—varied and distinctive. He created us equal in His love, but uniquely different in service for His kingdom. The Bible reminds us that God's knowledge of us is so intimate that, as Jesus said, "Even the very hairs on your head are numbered" (Matthew 10:30). Psalm 139:14 reminds us that we are wonderfully made. Do you know the One Who has a purpose for your life? He loves you more than you can imagine. He will make known the plan for your life as you obey the prompting and guiding of the Holy Spirit. Just as shells are uniquely and wonderfully distinctive, so are you.

Heavenly Father, thank You for the perfect plan that You have for me. Through love and service to You, I pray that my life will reflect the unique reason for which I am created.

REFLECTIONS

His Healing Touch

He himself bore our sins in his body on the cross, so that we might die to sins and live for righteousness; by his wounds you have been healed. 1 Peter 2:24

IT WAS AN ideal day for walking the beach. The hot sun knew just where to ease the pain as it focused its life-giving rays into our winter weary bodies. My husband John and I playfully dodged the lapping waves as we walked along the edge of the water. We enjoyed this time, because we knew soon enough the frigid winter would return, holding us again in its frosty fingers. It seemed we could walk forever, allowing ourselves to be united with God's powerful, yet healing forces.

Our eternal God is unchanging—the great I Am (Exodus 3:14). He is also Jehovah-Rapha which means in Hebrew, "I am the God who heals you." He is a healing and restorative God, whose loving nature intervenes in our physical difficulties. He created our bodies from the dust of the earth and knows every inch of us intimately. God may choose our healing through physicians, surgeons, changed health choices, or a direct miraculous touch. He may help us endure our physical suffering, take us through to our complete healing, or provide perfect healing in a new eternal body. The way He chooses is meant to perfect us spiritually and bring glory to Himself. While His methods and timing may be different than what we expect, God's love is certain; He wants only the best for us.

Are you resting in that love? Feel His healing touch as you walk the shores of life with Him. He will never let go. If you have pulled your hand away, He hasn't left you. Just reach out again and take hold. Isaiah 30:18 says, "The Lord longs to be gracious to you; therefore he will rise up to show you compassion. Blessed are all who wait for him!"

Thank You, Lord, that through Your nail-scarred hands, You deliver comfort and declare, "Do not fear. I will never leave you. Hold my hand while I walk with You today."

REFLECTIONS

Out of the Pit

He brought me up also out of a horrible pit, out of the miry clay, and set my feet upon a rock, and established my goings. Psalm 40:2 (KJV)

"WOW, THAT CHILD is digging a deep hole," I mentioned to my husband, as we watched him flinging sand everywhere. He worked for hours in the afternoon sun, sinking deeper with every shovelful of sand, until we could see only his head and shoulders. Why all this effort and focus on a shoreline pit? Maybe he loved excavating, or perhaps he thought the sand would yield a precious treasure. Whatever the reason, he was investing many hours in the job, and finally when he tired his dad reached down to lift him out. The sandy crater was abandoned, and later that evening as we walked the beach, we had to be watchful to not tumble in.

Early the next morning, we noticed that the recovering sand from the night tide had filled the cavity, eliminating evidence of the child's previous project. It was just as if the sand had never been disturbed.

In Psalm 40, a messianic prophecy, God reveals to David and the reader the answer for the pits that we fall into—Our Savior, Jesus Christ. Life is not struggle free, and sometimes we are challenged by the consequences of sin, emotional distress, or physical illness. But just as David laments the pit he was in, he rejoices that he knows the Rescuer "who heard his cry" (vs.1).

As the tide washes over sand and levels it once again, God's grace covers our sin and smoothes over our transgressions when we seek deliverance. He is compassionate and gracious, slow to anger, and abounding in love (vs.8). Philippians 1:6 reminds us that God began a good work in us and will be faithful to complete it.

If you have been a pit-dweller recently, rejoice! Help is on the way. If not, rejoice, as well. Jesus is beside you to keep your foot from slipping.

Gracious Lord Jesus, You are the Deliverer when I see no way up from life's darkest pit. Thank You for saving me from destruction and setting my feet on solid ground again.

REFLECTIONS

_____

_____

_____

_____

_____

_____

_____

_____

_____

_____

_____

_____

_____

_____

_____

_____

_____

_____

Dolphin Play

Come near to God and he will come near to you.
James 4:8

DOLPHINS— REMARKABLE, BEAUTIFUL, graceful creations of God. We walk by the seashore at sunrise to catch a glimpse of their sleek, powerful bodies, rising just barely above the ocean's surface. As they glide along, breaching the surface, we imagine the play and joyful bonding taking place within the dolphin world. They swim so effortlessly along the horizon of our sight, bringing a sense of safety to the water's mysteries and perhaps even protection from more fearsome ocean inhabitants. We grab our binoculars— spotting even one would make our day. Seeing a dolphin calf would be a wonder, but they have their own agenda for their dolphin hours. How marvelous it would be if they could send a friendly whisper or playful thought our way. If they could just hear our delight toward them and catch us in their excellent line of vision. We fantasize hearing their click-click-clicking dolphin words echoing back delight at our notice of them.

God longs for us to feel that same delight and awe in His presence. In return He seeks to demonstrate His friendship, joy, and care toward us, if we will come near to Him. Unlike the dolphin, He is not illusive. We don't have to view Him from a distance. He is always near and is our Worthy Protector. God reminds us that He has proven His presence in the person of Jesus. He has provided for our every need, but especially for our eternity with Him. He is as close as a prayer. We don't have to look from a distance. Do you see Him?

Father, the wonder of Your presence fills our hearts. Thank You for reminding us through the beauty of the magnificent dolphin how much we long to see and know You. Thank You, too, for providing a way to come near, through our Savior, Jesus Christ.

REFLECTIONS

Smooth Stones

The weapons we fight with are not the weapons of the world. On the contrary, they have divine power to demolish strongholds. 2 Corinthians 10:4

YOU MAY MISS them if you are not looking—beautifully polished beach stones. My husband's name for them is "butter beans," because of the resemblance. They boast colors like alabaster white, marbled black, or variegated brown. Their charm is often ignored in deference to unique shells, as they rest nestled in sand and seaweed. If the sunlight is focused perfectly, some may advertise their presence by a glittering gemstone or mineral encased. When displayed in a lovely container they possess a distinctive beauty wrought by wave action and weathering. Where have they been; how far have they come? These questions have a fascinating appeal to stone collectors who value them for art or jewelry.

Do you remember a Bible story about an important stone? 1 Samuel 17 relates the account of the shepherd boy David and his battle against the formidable Philistine warrior Goliath. There was much to fear, including every inch of Goliath's nine foot stature and his twenty pound sword. But as Goliath placed his faith in the external, young David picked out a smooth stone from his bag, and under God's guidance, defeated the giant who struck fear into the Israelite army. With faith in God David went forth empowered.

Do you have giants to conquer today? Remember that the power to do so does not come from what you possess, but from the One Who holds you.

Thank You God that You are all I need today to conquer any giant that comes my way. I trust You with all that I am.

REFLECTIONS

Paths to the Sea

(Be) rooted and built up in him, strengthened in the faith as you were taught, and overflowing with thankfulness. Colossians 2:7

SEA OATS, UNIOLA panicula, with deep roots, are the strong sentinels of the beach as they line the sand dunes. Through storms and terrifying hurricanes they remain on duty, guarding and protecting like little sandy soldiers. They root down and anchor themselves tenaciously to courser sand and sediments that are blown against them. In fact, the more they are surrounded with abrasive deposits, the faster they grow and spread. Despite what is thrown against sea oats, they thrive with a gentle, swaying beauty, as they proudly present the path to the restless ocean.

In Matthew 13:1-9 and 18-25, Jesus told a parable about the farmer who scatters his seed. The seed landed in four types of ground—but only the good ground allowed the seed to produce a worthy crop. Jesus reminds us that the outcome of our lives depends on the condition of our heart's soil. Are we allowing the Bible to be the strong sentinel, the guardian, of our heart? Are we as tenaciously rooted in our faith as the sea oats are in the sand? Is the harsh sediment of trials deepening our dependence on God?

If so, we can look forward to an abundant yield of blessings for ourselves and others as the Lord works in our lives. When you see sea oats today, thank God for His presence and work in your life.

Thank you Lord for every lesson we learn through Your creation. May our hearts be rooted in You.

REFLECTIONS

Game On!

I am the vine; you are the branches. If you remain in me and I in you, you will bear much fruit; apart from me you can do nothing. John15:5

BEACH COMPETITIONS ARE always popular. I am a gold medal winner at beach chair sitting while watching others play games as seriously as Olympians. In the heat of the day they play their favorites—maybe the fast moving, classic volleyball, slower, more precise Italian bocce ball, or colorful ladder golf. Some players are very aggressive and love to make a contest out of any game, and others play just for the joy of being with friends or family. Whether watching or playing, contests bring a few hours of freedom from more serious life battles and the game faces we wear in public.

More critical games are played, however, with our relationship to God. We may try to appease God by being religious without seeking a genuine relationship. We think we are doing God a favor by showing up at church or speaking righteous words. We might try games like salvation by works or my own priorities come before God's will for me. We don't want to be obligated beyond what we think will guarantee heaven.

Playing games with God brings disobedience and only that which perishes. If we love God we spend time in prayer, asking Him to help us live for that which is eternal. As we are grafted onto His team, we bear the fruit of victory through the Holy Spirit's indwelling. Let's play on the winning side today.

Lord, forgive me when I waste time playing games with You. Thank You that when I trust You I am on the side of the One Who obtained my victory at Calvary.

REFLECTIONS

Beyond the Horizon

Dear friends, now we are children of God, and what we will be has not yet been made known. But we know that when Christ appears, we shall be like him, for we shall see him as he is. 1 John 3:2

CAN YOU PICTURE the ocean beyond the horizon, where sky appears to join the water? We can only imagine how busy the ocean is. Binoculars may bring some of the action into focus, but so much more is occurring. Maritime ships move precious cargo along the shipping lanes, and commercial fishing boats trawl for a robust haul of the sea's delicacies. Channel markers bob up and down guiding vessels to safety, while sand is mined to replenish beaches. Coral reefs are being formed; water birds and marine life care for their young. Communication cables are laid across miles, while dangerous storms form.

The Bible reminds us that we see only partially what life is about and God's plans for those who love Him. 1 Corinthians 13: 12 states, "For now we see only a reflection as in a mirror; then we shall see face to face. Now I know in part; then I shall know fully, even as I am fully known." Life here is just a shadow of what God has prepared for us in eternity. Today we see only through our spiritual binoculars what He allows, but we know one day we will behold the incredible inheritance He has planned (1Peter 1:4).

For those who don't know Christ, the future brings a frightening reality. Let's watch, prepare, and share Him with others in anticipation of that day when we will see our Lord face to face—beyond the horizon.

Lord, thank You for the assurance that one day I will see more than just this partial view. I know on that day I will look upon Your face, see the nail prints in Your hands, and realize that despite my limited vision, You have always had an eternal plan for me, prepared from the foundation of the world.

REFLECTIONS

The Anchor Holds

We have this hope as an anchor for the soul, firm and secure. Hebrews 6:19

"ALL ABOARD!" CAPTAIN Dave bellowed, as he checked off his passenger log. We were headed for a day of open water fishing on Angler's Edge, his forty-two foot vessel. As we pulled out from harbor's safely, I watched as he carefully directed the craft toward the open water, then I settled in for the ride. I took stock of what was onboard—navigational instruments, a huge cooler for the day's catch, fishing gear, snacks, and drinks. A more significant and crucial provision, however, was the heavy impressive-looking anchor that would secure our position at his favorite fishing spot and provide stability against sudden turbulence. Captain Dave knew just how to cast it into the seabed for firm placement, so I felt safe on this adventure.

The apostle Paul reminds us that if we know Jesus Christ as our Savior, we have an Anchor Who secures our soul through the worst of tempests. He offers hope that the world cannot provide. Though the waters may be rough and storms threaten, we are safe since His promises never change. Because of what Jesus has done for us through His sacrificial death and resurrection, He anchors us for eternity.

Dear Lord, keep me anchored in You. I know that You have a perfect plan for me. When I place my hope in You I won't be disappointed in the Vessel in which I sail.

REFLECTIONS

_____

_____

_____

_____

_____

_____

_____

_____

_____

_____

_____

_____

_____

_____

_____

_____

_____

_____

_____

_____

In the Rear View Mirror

Because God has said, "Never will I leave you; never will I forsake you."

Hebrews 13:5

"NANA, COULD WE go down to the beach one more time before we leave?" our granddaughter Abbey asked, as we were busy packing for our trip home.

"Yes—please!" our grandson Brennan chimed in. I felt the same way. Our ocean refuge provides clarity and tranquility we often miss in daily life. The urgency of schedules is forgotten in the freedom of living in the moment.

"Good idea," I replied, as we grabbed the sunscreen for one last walk before our farewell to ocean's majesty. As my husband and I watched the children run ahead, I praised God for this time in His place.

Finally, as we crossed the sand dunes with our back to the water, the sea oats waved their goodbyes. We breathed in the warm salty air, and as we drove off I took one last look in the rear view mirror, thanking God for His marvelous creation. We will always have a yearning for the water's edge.

In the same way, we may leave God's presence by filling our lives with other things and holding on to that which distracts us from Him. But when the world doesn't satisfy we long to return to His loving embrace, for He has built into us an innate desire to connect. Just as we want to tarry at the beach, so we want to linger in His presence. Ecclesiastes 3:11 states, "He has set eternity in the human heart." God longs for our return with great anticipation and arms outstretched. We can return at any moment; He has never left. See Him waiting?

Dear Lord, I admit that I love Your creation, especially the beauty of the water's edge where my spirit finds peace. But it is also a place that reminds me that there is peace in staying in Your embrace and will for my life. I thank You that Your love for me is deeper than the ocean, and Your thoughts about me are more numerous than the grains of sands on the beach (Psalm 139:18).

REFLECTIONS

Dear Reader,

I pray that as you have read these devotions and reflected on God in the beauty of His creation your faith has deepened, and you have been drawn into a closer relationship with Him. Remember that as you look to God, He keeps watchful care over you. However, if you do not know the God of this universe intimately, you can. He has provided a way through his Son, Jesus Christ. You can put your faith in Christ for the abundant and eternal life He wants you to have. Here's how:

1. We are all separated from God until we recognize our need to be reconciled to Him. Agreeing with God that you are a sinner allows Him to work in your life. Admit your need, confess your sin, and let God begin a wonderful work in your heart.
2. Through prayer, invite Jesus to come into your heart for salvation, forgiveness and reconciliation.
3. Turn from your sins. We call this repentance.
4. Put your faith and trust in Him to direct your future.

When you have done this you are promised salvation. You are promised life with Him here and eternal life with Him after death. We have today; tomorrow is not assured. Now is the time. May you experience the joy of knowing God and living in His presence daily.

Barbara Baranowski

About the Author

Barbara Baranowski is a retired middle school teacher, writer, and inspirational speaker devoted to family, educational, and spiritual issues. She lives with her husband John in Roanoke, Virginia, where she directs Roanoke Valley Christian Writers. Barbara has enjoyed the beach for many years with her family. She is an experienced camper, as well, and whether spending a week in a beach home, camping in the mountains, or enjoying breathtaking scenery wherever she travels, Barbara seeks to glorify God because of His handiwork throughout creation and within her life. She is the first to acknowledge that Jesus Christ is the true Author of *In God's Creation, Devotions for the Beach* and should receive any credit due.

Barbara is also the author of *In God's Creation, Devotions for the Outdoors,* available through WestBow Publishing and Amazon. Check out her website at www.inspiredsenior.org.

Printed in the United States
By Bookmasters